NICK INGLIS

ADVANCING FROM EDISCOVERY TO PREDISCOVERY

InfoGov.net
217 Whitford Ave
Providence, RI 02908

Contents

PREDISCOVERY

For my son and wife, who've endured years of conversations where I attempted to succinctly explain what I do for a living. - Nick

FOREWORD

Over the past decade, we've seen two major trends gain significant acceleration in the information profession— 1) Information Governance (IG) is becoming pervasive, and 2) eDiscovery has become ever more reliant on advanced technology and agile infrastructure.

Importantly, these functions have increasingly begun to converge. Whereas previously the systems, processes, and people tended to approach issues separately, today we see that companies, law firms, and service providers that have decided to embrace this convergence are reaping significant operational and economic benefits.

In this book, Nick articulates a plan for how leading organizations can harness the benefits of combining IG and eDiscovery. Early adopters of the concepts he outlines here are already seeing a tremendous impact on:

- lowered risk and costs
- optimized information environments
- improved compliance and security, and
- dramatically faster data insights.

With a massive explosion of data that began well before the pandemic,concerns around global privacy and compliance, and the ever-present threat of breaches, the convergence of IG and eDiscovery is not only timely but essential.

Given this landscape, it is necessary for us, across multiple disciplines and data stacks, to determine how to best approach the critical alignment of our information disciplines.

At IPRO, we develop software spanning eDiscovery and Information Governance to help facilitate a new unified method to understand all this data. We've not only embraced the convergence Nick outlines, we proactively enable it in organizations by providing the technology that can create and facilitate this interdisciplinary alignment.

The most effective organizations we've seen adopt this approach are actively leveraging IG tools and processes to gain insights "upstream". This knowledge—everything from the topography to rights to entities—can directly feed a more efficient, managed discovery process.

But the benefits require a cohesive insight into your data and a truly integrated approach to governance, risk, compliance, and discovery.

Our software supports the concepts you'll read about in this book across the eDiscovery and Information Governance spectrum, providing the invisible data automation required for compliant and secure stewardship of your informational assets in a way that reduces risk while creating lasting economic value.

I am thankful to have Nick as IPRO's Director of Information Governance (in addition to his work at InfoGov.net, which we also greatly applaud). We're forging ahead into this bold future while enabling the "upstream" thinking required to help transform and modernize traditional approaches.

We are proud to sponsor this book's authorship and help unleash these concepts for our clients and partners worldwide.

Dean Brown
CEO, IPRO

SECTION I: INTRODUCTION

"If we are to better the future, we must disturb the present."
- Catherine Booth, Co-Founder, The Salvation Army

INTRODUCTION

PreDiscovery?

The title of this book is "Advancing from eDiscovery to PreDiscovery," which alludes to some discipline called "*PreDiscovery*" out there. While I don't expect "PreDiscovery" to be a term that we start adding into our lexicons, I think it's an accurate descriptor of the role that Information Governance must play as a part of our eDiscovery process as we advance. Information Governance represents the work that must go into eDiscovery before we ever start talking about an individual case - thus, PreDiscovery is in the title. Don't go around trying to make "PreDiscovery" a term that we're all going to start using; I don't want that - none of us want that.

■■

Additional Resources

To access additional resources from this book, including a reader community, graphics, templates, and more, visit https://myigl.ink/prediscovery or scan the QR code on the following page.

Information Governance

Information Governance is a relatively young professional discipline. It was just in 2010 that then-Gartner analyst, Debra Logan, defined the term Information Governance. Since then, the term "Information Governance" and the newly formed underlying discipline have expanded rapidly.

From Gartner, "Information governance is the specification of decision rights and an accountability framework to encourage desirable behavior in the valuation, creation, storage, use, archival and deletion of information. It includes the processes, roles, standards, and metrics that

PREDISCOVERY

ensure the effective and efficient use of information in enabling an organization to achieve its goals."[1]

While I appreciate Logan's definition, I prefer the definition that I created, which now serves as the definition at ARMA International, "Information governance is the overarching and coordinating strategy for all organizational information. It establishes the authorities, supports, processes, capabilities, structures, and infrastructure to enable information to be a useful asset and reduced liability to an organization, based on that organization's specific business requirements and risk tolerance."[2]

Both definitions position Information Governance as the highest level of guidance for all organizational information. Information Governance is situated directly underneath Corporate Governance and reflects corporate governance (as explicitly applied to the organization's information). For the visual learners like myself, I created two helpful graphics to represent organizations both without and with Information Governance to illustrate how there are distributed and, likely, inconsistent points of information-related decision-making spread throughout an organization without IG (Fig 1.1).

The "*with* Information Governance" version of the visual (Fig 1.2) shows how IG is seated in an organization to centralize

---

[1] https://blogs.gartner.com/debra_logan/2010/01/11/what-is-information-governance-and-why-is-it-so-hard/

[2] https://www.arma.org/page/Information_Governance

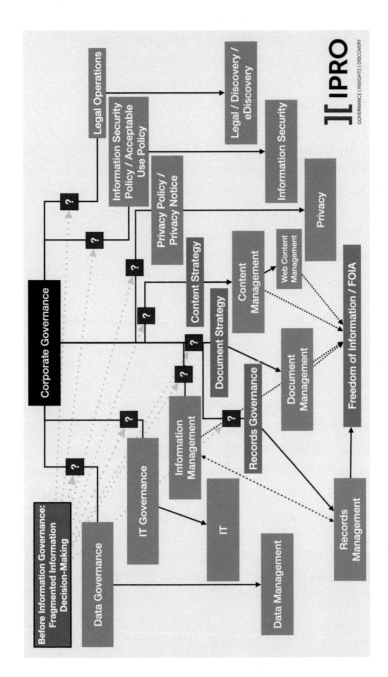

Fig 1.1: *Without* Information Governance

information-related decision-making and ensure consistency in policy, practice, and process.

Information Governance is the umbrella discipline that situates itself above all other information-related disciplines and aligns their efforts. In this situating above other fields, we've seen some organizations struggle - it was challenging for some organizations to situate a new domain with less maturity above multiple disciplines with solid maturity.

The early adopters came prepared to challenge those presumptions with results - Information Governance works. We started sharing with one another at the conference I'd co-founded, the first of its kind in the information governance space. I created a model that was put into use in over a quarter of the Fortune 500, now called the ARMA Information Governance Implementation Model (IGIM).

In those early adopter companies, we saw incredible benefits from IG. Many were published and distributed as case studies by associations such as ACEDS, AIIM, ARMA, AHIMA, EDRM, ILTA, Information Coalition, and others. Many other case studies, white papers, and briefings came from software vendors, with some business-oriented periodicals like Forbes pushing Information Governance.[3, 4, 5]

---

[3] https://www.ciosummits.com/CEO-WP-Series-Information-Governance.pdf

[4] http://library.ahima.org/doc?oid=107466#.YK5oppNKjel

[5] https://www.forbes.com/sites/riskmap/2015/06/01/the-many-blessings-of-information-governance/?sh=a8abe301a8a9

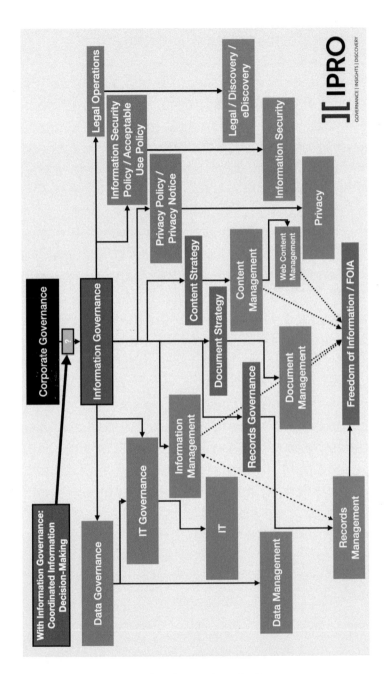

Fig 1.2: *With* Information Governance

From those early benefits, we've seen rapid expansion. Project Management took nearly two decades to gain recognition as a discipline (starting in the 60s); IG has risen to the highest echelons of organizations in under 10 years. We've seen this rapid adoption because of three factors:

1. Executives are increasingly viewing information as an organizational asset as valuable as money.[6]

2. Early adopters of Information Governance were open in sharing their wins and benefits (thanks to early trailblazers for sharing your results in those early gatherings of the Information Governance Conference[7]).

3. Information Governance makes logical sense - there was a need, and we created a discipline to fill that need.

That rapid adoption has meant, though, that companies of all sizes are at various stages of maturity when it comes to their Information Governance programs. There are large companies with incredibly mature programs applying technologies to automate parts of the IG programs. Meanwhile, there are also large companies that are just

---

[6] https://www.gartner.com/smarterwithgartner/why-every-business-should-be-an-information-business/

[7] Of particular note: Judy Selby (BakerHostetler LLP); Matt McClelland (Blue Cross Blue Shield of NC); Jeffrey D. Bridges (Boehringer Ingelheim USA); Alexander Campbell & Leslie Lewis (Cohen & Gresser, LLC); Russel Walters (Johnson & Johnson); Stephen Cohen (MetLife); Leigh Isaacs (Orrick, Herrington, & Sutcliffe, LLP); Jessica Harmon (Philips66); Linn Freedman (Robinson+Cole LLP); William Tong (State of Connecticut); Richard Kessler (UBS); Jeff Kosseff (US Naval Academy); Joel Westphal (US Navy); and Aaron Crews (Walmart).

getting started today. There are more large companies on the mature side of the scale than smaller ones, but companies of all sizes are across all maturity levels.[8]

If you already have an IG program, you'll benefit from this book in understanding the changes you'll need to make to maximize the benefits of alignment with eDiscovery. If you don't already have an IG program, you'll learn how to start a program already aligned with eDiscovery successfully.

■■

eDiscovery

Contrasting to the history of Information Governance, eDiscovery is a mature discipline borne out of paper-based Discovery.

eDiscovery rose to prominence as email rose to prominence. Judges and lawyers quickly realized that natively digital email was just as relevant (if not more so) than the volumes of paper produced related to legal cases.

There were many growing pains (all laid bare in court proceedings) in the early days of eDiscovery, and many questions had very unclear answers early on:

---

[8] https://www.arma.org/page/ig-report

- How would information be produced digitally?
- How can you represent a threaded conversation as it exists in email?
- What is discoverable, and what must be produced?

All these questions and more were addressed through seminal cases such as Zubulake v. UBS Warburg (the multiple decisions issued by Judge Shira Scheindlin, more affectionately: Zubulake I, Zubulake III, Zubulake IV, and Zubulake V); incredibly thoughtful decisions also came from Judge Andrew Peck, Judge Ronald Hedges, Judge Paul Grimm, and Judge John Facciola, while Judge Lee Rosenthal deserves credit for pushing 2006's Amendments to the Federal Rules of Civil Procedure and defining how to produce ESI in civil litigation.

We stand on the shoulders of giants in making further advancements in eDiscovery. This book will not be looking at individual cases, judges, or rulings and their impacts on eDiscovery (that's the work of the lawyers in our space and I'm a technologist and strategist), but instead will be looking at the underlying processes used to enable eDiscovery in alignment with the law.

eDiscovery, the digital counterpart of paper-based Discovery has spent nearly all of its existence dealing with one constant is change. As soon as a decision has firmed one area of confusion in the realm of eDiscovery, a new technology or challenge emerges to take its' place.

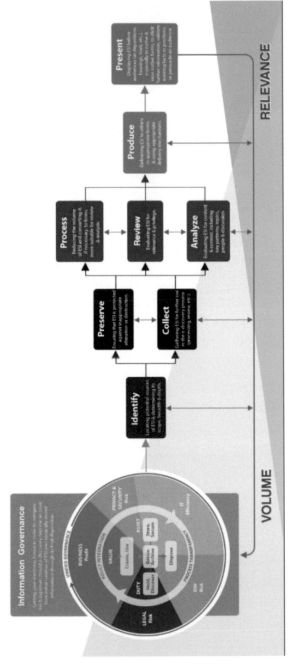

Fig 1.3: EDRM

I raise this point to those who are resistant to the assumption that eDiscovery itself must change - of course it must change, it hasn't stopped changing since its inception.

██

This Book

This approach we'll be discussing in this book: how to drive connection and enhance the information environment for significant improvement in both Information Governance and eDiscovery. We'll look at improvements across both disciplines and where those benefits fall beyond the two. We'll also look at the guidance for the professionals who orchestrate information optimization in your organization.

While I recognize that no two companies or law firms, or service providers, are the same, there are significant commonalities in the processes when we bring the two disciplines together. The goal is so engrained, that EDRM (the organization) updated the currently dominant model in eDiscovery, the EDRM (the model). The current version of the dominant model for eDiscovery provides a visual representation of eDiscovery that now includes a solid nod to the discipline of Information Governance.

██

Issues with EDRM

I like the EDRM Model, but I do have some issues with it. The primary issue I take with this model isn't that it isn't valid - the EDRM model is an entirely accurate understanding and viewpoint for both eDiscovery and Information Governance. The problem I find with the model is a disjointed *perspective* between the two disciplines represented in the model. The lenses used to look at eDiscovery and Information Governance are actually two different lenses - neither is invalid, but they are inconsistent - which adds confusion.

On the eDiscovery side of the model, you see a process-oriented view of eDiscovery. The model walks you through the specific steps that you'd take in an eDiscovery project. That is incredibly helpful and has allowed eDiscovery to mature with some grounding on a consistent workflow process. As you'll see in my look at the future of eDiscovery, I believe it's time to update the underlying process.

On the Information Governance side of the model, you see not a process-oriented view, but a stakeholder-oriented view of Information Governance. It shows the primary stakeholders and a descriptor of how those stakeholders connect. It gives some clues as to the processes underlying

IG, but it is very far from the straightforward process provided on the eDiscovery side of the model.

That said, the fact that any eDiscovery model was recognizing the need for Information Governance was a huge leap forward at the time. That recognition allowed for Information Governance to flourish, but the disconnect between the sides of the model were limiting.

Given this disconnect, no wonder that there is so much misunderstanding in the eDiscovery space of what Information Governance is (let alone what it is trying to achieve). Likewise, while IG professionals frequently cite stakeholders to Information Governance, very few professionals on the IG side are utilizing the model to run their IG program - it just isn't prescriptive in the same ways as the eDiscovery portion is.

■■

A Point on Costs

In the EDRM process, the greater the distance becomes between the stages of Collect and Analyze, the higher the costs will be to the client. If you're the client, you probably hate this and it likely makes you feel uneasy - if you're the law firm or service provider, it might make you a bit uncomfortable that you're profiting without as much transparency as you'd like to provide. This cost containment issue is likely to face future scrutiny.

■■

A Point on Paper

As noted several times during the brief explanations of the stages of the EDRM - paper remains prominent as an indicator of the process. It is these paper-oriented processes that we must evaluate for efficiency, as we don't live in a paper-based world any longer - we're in a digital world.

■■

A Point on Massive File Transfers

As someone who was first a technologist, then an expert in Information Governance and eDiscovery, what shocked and horrified me about the process is the massive amounts of information (as files) that are shipped off to other companies (law firms, service providers, consultants). In no other information-related discipline would this even remotely be considered an acceptable practice, and I'll state it plainly: massive file transfers shouldn't be a common practice in the world of eDiscovery either.

It's all about risk management- when a company is not in control of its information, it is relying on third parties to uphold their obligations on information handling - that introduces one level of risk, albeit a slight chance if all agreements with the firm include an agreeable section on information handling practices.

The more significant risk, though, has to do with law firms themselves. Law firms and healthcare providers are now at the top of hackers' (and other bad actors') lists as targets for their nefarious activities. The reason for the two sectors is precisely the same - when you're attacking one, you're attacking many. With healthcare providers, you're not just hacking the healthcare provider; you're attacking every patient of the healthcare provider. With law firms, you're not just hacking a law firm; you're attacking all of the companies with information held at the firm (and that often includes past clients who haven't worked with the firm in what may be decades whose information may still reside at the firm).

We have to stop massive file transfers; they're increasing our risks and costs as a profession. We need to keep privacy and security at the top of mind when we reimagine the parts of the process that generally rely on large file transfers.

■■

Model Forward

Upon joining the team at IPRO (March 2021), I set to work in trying to create a new model for our clients that reflects a future vision in the near-term. This new model must be process-oriented throughout - to understand the specific steps that professionals take to approach their goals. We must modernize this new model based on the technological advancements of the past decade.

The eDiscovery portion of the EDRM has barely changed over the past two decades, and no one believes that the technology underlying the discipline has remained nearly as constant as the model. The EDRM also remains fully aligned with paper-based processes, where a professional can only perform a single task at a single point in time. Paper is very unlike digital assets. With a digital asset, we can, by applying technology, perform multiple steps on a single digital asset or numerous digital assets at a time. That will allow us to collapse many of the time-consuming stages of the EDRM into a shorter, more well-defined (and more linear) process.

■■

Let's Be Clear - EDRM is Still Great

All of this to say, the EDRM, while a valid and valuable tool in the arsenal of any IG or eDiscovery professional, is not the forward-operating model of this book - it serves as a point of informing, but not something upon which we can make further progress in eDiscovery or Information Governance without revision. I expect we'll see future revision of the EDRM look a lot like some of the ideas proposed within this book.

The EDRM remains the dominant model in our space, and it is likely to remain so - it is by questioning everything that we'll likely see the EDRM updated later to reflect many of the tenets that we're discussing in this book today.

A quick point here, EDRM is both a model *and* an underlying thought-leadership organization: the thought-leadership organization is genuinely top-notch, and they're discussing many of the topics enclosed within this book, but their constituency spans the entire bell curve of adoption - from the early adopters, the folks who'll benefit the most from this book, through to the late adopters, the folks who'll wait it out and who'll read this book a decade from now. EDRM has to maintain its model for both audiences and talk to future advancements. In this book, however, I'll be driving ahead into what's currently happening in eDiscovery and IG, as well as what is very likely to come next.

■■

This Book's Approach

As a starting point, In part 1 of this book, we will look at the current state of Information Governance. Here I'm going to evaluate our current models for Information Governance, identifying weaknesses and process challenges that we're experiencing as a profession. We'll then look at the technology landscape and identify many of the projects being run under the banner of Information Governance to evaluate what processes exist as a part of Information Governance that might give us clues as to what a process-oriented vision of Information Governance might look like. After this thorough evaluation, we'll rethink our approach to Information Governance into a new process-oriented view.

Once we've evaluated Information Governance, we'll shift gears in Part 2 to follow the same 'Current State – Process Evaluation – Future State' framing with eDiscovery. First, we will look at the current state of eDiscovery. Here I'm going to give it an honest evaluation, looking at challenges and identifying weaknesses. We'll be looking at challenges and weaknesses in light of other sub-disciplines (e.g., privacy, security, business process management) as well as organizational efficiency and overall efficacy.

Next, we'll evaluate the potential for technology to perform various stages within the standard eDiscovery process, eliminating the stage (or the intervention of a human in the stage). That is what is allowing innovative companies and firms to gain new efficiencies in their eDiscovery processes.

Leveraging those insights, we'll propose a revamped eDiscovery process: one that leverages modern technology and aligns overall eDiscovery strategy, not to paper, but to digital information.

In Part 3, having reoriented the underlying processes of both disciplines, we'll look at the inflection points *between* the fields and techniques, evaluate the impact of the changes, and identify further areas of efficiency that we can gain by aligning the two professions. This section is where we'll draw the two disciplines together into closer alignment. Here is where I get the most excited about this work. By restructuring both fields and aligning their processes, we're able to drive additional efficiencies that had, to this point, been unattainable. I've already identified one new key process that can be gleaned through better alignment but I expect many others will be discovered.

This final section of the book will present the fully aligned and new unified eDiscovery/PreDiscovery (eD/PD) model. This approach, I believe, is scalable well into the future and will hopefully become the operating model for innovative companies and law firms around the world.

■■

My Biases

It would be unfair for me to write a book declaring a new path forward without addressing the personal biases that I bring to this work. Firstly, I'm an Information Governance professional - while I'm deeply knowledgeable about eDiscovery and widely considered a leading thought-leader in both disciplines; it is Information Governance where I find my deepest professional grounding.

I am a technologist and **not** a lawyer (so don't take any of this as legal advice, **this book isn't legal advice**) - I came to the broader information profession first as a web and software developer, and my career has expanded from those beginnings. I have led the SharePoint program and then later the entire Professional Development department at AIIM International. After which, I co-founded and led the Information Coalition over several years (now part of ARMA International) and led all thought leadership for ARMA International as their Executive Director of Content & Programming.

I co-founded the first conference exclusively focused on Information Governance and built an organization underlying the conference to drive thought leadership in the space, called the Information Coalition (and the aptly named, "Information Governance Conference"). It was this group and the underlying conference that ARMA International acquired. After the acquisition through ARMA International, I continued that thought leadership with a deep focus on Information Governance and Records Management (the legacy of ARMA International).

These experiences in leading the direction of professional associations in the information space have brought me into contact with companies of all shapes and sizes, offering guidance and analyzing results. From this, I bring a deep knowledge of technology, process, and information management - as understood through the lens of Enterprise Content Management - a concept championed by AIIM International that has now morphed into the idea of Intelligent Information Management.

Today, I serve in multiple roles. Firstly, at IPRO, I serve as the Director of Information Governance in a public-facing and internal thought-leadership role. In addition, I founded InfoGov.net to build the capacity for lobbying in the Information Governance profession, and am currently hosting a podcast on the platform called "The Strategy of Information".

Further, this book and its resulting model aren't my first book or my first effort at creating a model in the information space - this is my third book, and I've created several models in my time serving in the information space. My first book, "The SharePoint 2010 Governance Toolkit," also included a model within it - the AIIM International SharePoint Governance Model. That model was a governance framework specifically designed for SharePoint 2010 - a helpful framework used in companies worldwide. The trend moved towards many organizations implementing Microsoft SharePoint 2010 and struggling to maintain control of the information within the new technology. While that particular model has lost its' usefulness over the years as the technology was deprecated and replaced with more recent versions, it was incredibly helpful in informing my subsequent model work. "INFORMATION: The Comprehensive Overview of the Information Profession" was my second work, and it remains available through ARMA International as a definitive guide to the various disciplines and elements utilized throughout the broader information profession, and it has helped to create a shared understanding of many core concepts and ideas that we can share between information-related disciplines.

During my time leading the Information Coalition, I created the Information Governance Model, which after acquisition became the ARMA International Information Governance Implementation Model (IGIM), which lives on today at ARMA International. That model has become one of the leading models in Information Governance and serves as ARMA International's basis for their annual IG Maturity Index Survey and Report. The IGIM is an implementation-focused model (an important distinction that we'll reevaluate) used to establish an Information Governance program and benchmark IG efforts. Benchmarking using the IGIM leverages companies worldwide based on the IG Maturity Index Survey and Report results as tracked over time. At the time of publication, there have been two reports, with benchmarking work based on that already-captured data underway at ARMA International. All of this work continues to be made available through ARMA International at https://www.arma.org/igim.

We will discuss the IGIM model in this book and the EDRM model, as well as several others. The ARMA IGIM is a model that is currently utilized in thousands of companies worldwide and serves as the basis of Information Governance programs in companies, government agencies, law firms, and non-profit organizations; at last check, over 25% of the Fortune 500 were using the IGIM model or its' predecessors.

So, having already created a model in Information Governance, why didn't I simply use my previous modeling work for this new effort? Again, just like the EDRM, the IGIM is a different framing of the discipline - the IGIM is not a process-oriented view and can't serve as the basis of process alignment. It *is* helpful as we look at the current state of IG, and we will discuss it, but it won't serve as the foundation of this new work.

■■

Moving Forward

This book aims to enable companies and professionals in both disciplines to leverage this work to move forward - towards better working and improved efficiency. This chapter opened with a Catherine Booth quote which is the guiding principle for this work - this effort doesn't exist to disrupt either discipline, Information Governance, or eDiscovery. No one wants to disrupt aligning information efforts within organizations *(or the law)* - instead, this work seeks to disturb the present and prod information professionals (yes, lawyers are often information professionals too) into new ways of thinking about how we operate and find a new path forward, together, for both disciplines.

■■

Key Takeaways:

☐ Information Governance and eDiscovery are disciplines that are converging.

☐ Information Governance is the highest level of guidance for all organizational information.

☐ Information Governance is a relatively new profession.

☐ Information Governance is an umbrella discipline, situated above other information-related disciplines.

☐ eDiscovery is a mature discipline.

☐ eDiscovery was borne out of paper-based Discovery.

☐ EDRM is a model that shows the connection between eDiscovery and Information Governance.

☐ EDRM is an incredibly useful model.

☐ This book aims to drive better connection between the disciplines of eDiscovery and Information Governance.

SECTION II: INFORMATION GOVERNANCE

"We, as extremely complex creatures, desperately need to know this story of how the universe creates complexity and why complexity means vulnerability and fragility."
- David Christian

INFORMATION GOVERNANCE CURRENT STATE

Abysmal May Be Too Soft A Word

Let's face it, our handling of corporate information over the past two decades has been... *abysmal*. We've been inventing new technology *nearly* as fast as we've been able to understand how we can use the technology, protect the information that resides within the technology, and how it complies with applicable laws and regulations. Even more so than technology, the pace of information growth has far exceeded our capacity to manage every individual piece of information actively.

Our previous practices in organizing information by relying on human filing are simply unsustainable. Just think of the typical practices seen within shared drives - the 'wild west' of information repositories that *still* plague companies - and you will know that we need better ways of handling our information than, well, *that*.

In our recent past, we've attempted training and educating our way toward information betterment - we've spent money from our company war chests to teach the basic tenets of Information Management (really focusing on Records Management) and yet, study after study continues to find that employees continue to misfile a significant amount of information.

Today, issues stemming from the information explosion include:

☐ new privacy laws mandating that we understand how our organizations utilize personally identifiable information

☐ new security concerns from ransomware and hackers

☐ ongoing issues in simply searching and browsing for information

☐ the persistent threat of litigation.

How does any company possibly handle this myriad of problems without a plan? That plan is the approach of Information Governance (IG).

■■

Meet Information Governance

Information Governance is the newest discipline related to information, having existed for just over a decade. IG is an umbrella discipline that draws together the guidance of various information-related sub-disciplines that had previously been highly siloed and harmonizes them. Previous approaches presented inconsistencies in information practices; Information Governance provides a single organizational approach across ALL corporate information (including data). In Information Governance, you draw together the various information policies and practices that exist across your organization - harmonize the guidance while ensuring all policy is in alignment with organizational goals - and then drive information efficiencies forward (in conjunction with and in support of the various information sub-disciplines).

In an organizational structure chart, the flow of disciplines is (generally) as shown below:

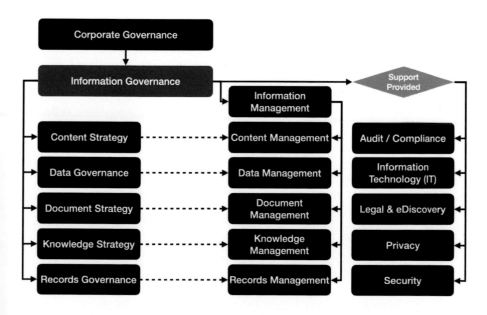

Fig 2.1: Information Governance among disciplines

All organizational guidance and policy should flow from and be consistent with Corporate Governance, and Information Governance should flow directly from Corporate Governance.

The terms "Governance" and "Strategy" are occasionally used interchangeably (as seen in the graphic above), but both convey a plan of action. Meanwhile, "Management" disciplines (e.g., Document Management, Knowledge Management, et al.) are the tactical execution of their respective Governance/Strategy discipline (where one doesn't exist in your organization, the guidance then stems directly from Information Governance, or in other cases, directly from Information Management - this depends on your organizational structure, as explained below).

Guidance flows from Information Governance to the various *strategic* sub-disciplines (Content Strategy, Data Governance, Document Strategy, Knowledge Strategy, and Records Governance [or any combination within your organization]). The guidance then flows in one of two ways for the *tactical* disciplines (Content Management, Data Management, Document Management, Knowledge Management, and Records Management [or any combination that exists within your organization]) -

1. Guidance may flow directly from the strategic counterpart to the tactical discipline (e.g., Document Management takes guidance from Document Strategy).
2. Guidance may flow from Information Governance, guidance translated from strategy into tactics by

PREDISCOVERY

Information Management, and then tactics are passed down to the tactical disciplines.

Both of these approaches can be successful and often depend on the individuals and relationships more than any specific benefits of taking either approach.

For example, in your organization, let's say there is no Records Governance function (as is frequently the case). In this scenario, Records Management would take guidance directly from either Information Governance or Information Management (depending on your organizational structure). Of note is that Information Management, itself, takes its direction from Information Governance (so there should be no inconsistencies, no matter which reporting structures you choose).

In addition to the disciplines that are frequently within the reporting structures, some disciplines can find support from Information Governance that don't *usually* have a direct reporting structure to Information Governance. Those disciplines are:

- Audit / Compliance
- Information Technology (IT)
- Legal & eDiscovery
- Privacy
- Security

Information Governance often ends up as a centralized point for supporting those other disciplines, often through either one-time projects (e.g., a privacy audit in support of the Privacy team) or through the application of ongoing automation (e.g., automated alerts on user permissions changes for the Security team, as that could be an indicator of a security issue).

■■

Upstream from eDiscovery

Information Governance is a growing discipline with more professionals entering the space regularly. With this expansion of professionals has come an expansion of collaboration between Information Governance and other information-related disciplines. The area of greatest collaborative growth right now is with eDiscovery. eDiscovery professionals are looking upstream towards the processes and disciplines that touch on information improvement to drive better downstream results in eDiscovery. As they look upstream they are finding a new burgeoning profession of Information Governance.

This book aims to harness this convergence of disciplines, looking upstream to achieve the best possible outcomes.

Key Takeaways

- [ ] Legacy information handling practices are unsustainable.
- [ ] Information Governance is the parent discipline to all information-related disciplines.
- [ ] "Governance" and "strategy" are often used interchangeably.
- [ ] Information Governance often supports Audit / Compliance, Information Technology (IT), Legal & eDiscovery, Privacy, and Security disciplines.
- [ ] Information Governance is upstream from eDiscovery.

INFORMATION GOVERNANCE PROCESS EVALUATION

The Model for Information Governance

In order to make improvements to the ways that we are currently operating, we have to look at the ways that we're currently operating. Our goal here is to understand the process that underlies Information Governance. When we understand the underlying process, we can look towards future improvement. In seeking to understand the process of Information, I turned towards the various models of Information Governance.

Many models exist for Information Governance exist, but we'll look at the three models in this volume:

- The EDRM's Information Governance Reference Model (IGRM)[9]

---

[9] https://edrm.net/resources/frameworks-and-standards/information-governance-reference-model/

- ARMA International's Information Governance Implementation Model (ARMA IGIM)[10]
- InfoGov.net Model for Information Governance (MIG)

Having created two of the three models examined here (ARMA IGIM & MIG), I feel like I have a unique vantage point for evaluating models for Information Governance, but clearly, I also bring a bit of bias into the discussion - be sure to consider all these models and any others that you find compelling.

	IGRM	IGIM	MIG
Stakeholder View	X	X	
Checklist View		X	
Project View		X	X
Process View			X

Fig 3.1: Comparison of vantage point of three IG models

■■

[10] https://www.arma.org/page/igim

EDRM's Information Governance Reference Model (IGRM)

The EDRM's Information Governance Reference Model (Fig 3.2) was a great leap forward for Information Governance. The IGRM was one of the first graphical representations of Information Governance, and it helped people grasp the concept of a multi-stakeholder information approach. Its pie-chart of disciplines helped to define Information Governance as a genuinely collaborative discipline. That EDRM created the IGRM, the creators of the wildly popular eDiscovery model, helped cement Information Governance as a concept that collaborated with eDiscovery. Later, the IGRM itself was appended to the beginning of the EDRM to show that Information Governance was necessary as a step before eDiscovery. The IGRM is a beautiful view into the stakeholders to Information Governance, and you can see references to policy, so you know there is policy involved in Information Governance. Likewise, in the center of the IGRM, a simple information lifecycle harkens to Information Management and Enterprise Content Management.

Since we're using a process evaluation to look at the flow of information between Information Governance and eDiscovery in this volume, we're going to need an IG framework that shows the steps that one should take to achieve Information Governance success, and on this point, we find the IGRM lacking. The IGRM wasn't ever intended to serve as a process-oriented view of Information Governance, so it is too high an expectation that it helps us

Information Governance Reference Model (IGRM)

v4.0 © 2021 EDRM.net

Fig 3.2: The EDRM Information Governance Reference Model (IGRM)

in this way.

So, what is the IGRM suitable for? Lots of things. Firstly, helping people to understand Information Governance through a stakeholder-oriented view is a great thing. Further, the IGRM has been the center of many C-suite conversations, and at that level, the IGRM is a phenomenal tool.

■■

ARMA Information Governance Implementation Model (IGIM)

The ARMA International Information Governance Implementation Model (Figs 3.3 & 3.4), or IGIM for short, was created by me (Nick Inglis) in 2013 (Steve Weissman also made significant contributions to the model). Originally called The Information Coalition Information Governance Model, it became the ARMA Information Governance Implementation Model when my organization, the Information Coalition, was acquired by ARMA International.

Initially, I created the model to help a consulting client that Steve Weissman and I were working with map out the elements of Information Governance into a cohesive view that we could share with executives (hive view, previous page) and information professionals alike (expanded view, next page). Our goal was to create a model that would

Fig 3.3 ARMA International Information Governance
Implementation Model - IGIM (Hive View)

assist us in creating a brand-new Information Governance program.

When we completed the consulting project, I realized I had something beneficial to many more companies than just the one. At this point, we released the first version of the Information Governance Model under an open-source license.

In the years immediately following our release and before our acquisition by ARMA International, the model had been downloaded thousands of times by people representing over half the Fortune 500.

After the ARMA acquisition, I helped transition the model to its new home, where it continues to help people establish brand new Information Governance programs. The model also underlies the Information Governance Maturity Index, the first large-scale benchmarking project for the profession.

The ARMA IGIM is a complex model - there are many boxes. Information Governance is complex, and for an elemental model of Information Governance, a complex model is necessary - there are many considerations in establishing an IG program.

For all the good that's come from the ARMA IGIM over the years, it made sense that we would turn to my prior work as a source of inspiration in evaluating Information Governance. Inspired, yes, but unfortunately, the model has the same Achilles' heel as the IGRM above; it is not a process-oriented view of Information Governance. So while the model is helpful for many use cases, it simply won't work for this use case.

■■

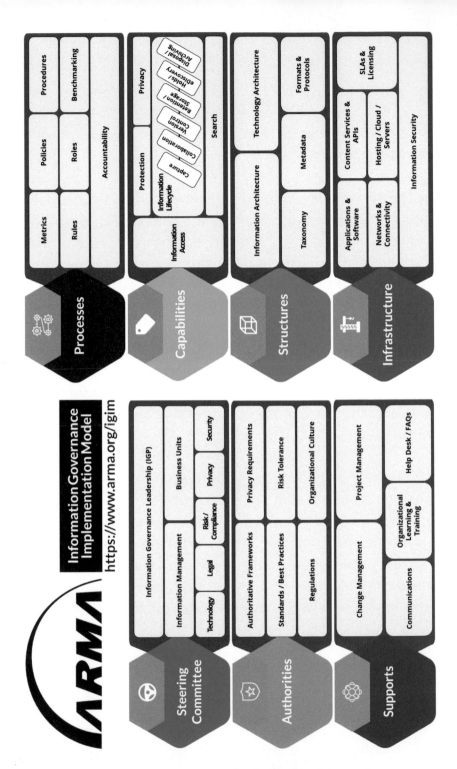

Fig 3.4 ARMA International Information Governance
Implementation Model - IGIM [expanded view]

Model for Information Governance (MIG)

I looked at many more models of Information Governance in a quest to find a process-oriented view of IG - needless to say, the investigation proved fruitless - and while I could dedicate a volume in evaluating the various models, I think this exercise has gone one quite long enough. Eventually, I threw in the towel and decided to create a new model, one that's focused on the process of Information Governance - the Model for Information Governance (MIG) is the fruit of that labor.

Fig 3.5 MIG Condensed

Everything in Information Governance fits quite nicely into just three linear boxes (compressed view). The first step in Information Governance is to align your program to your organization strategically. Next, Information Governance professionals often run a series of one-time projects, usually targeted at specific organizational challenges, sometimes in support of a sub-discipline's challenge. Lastly, as programs mature, you start to see more activity in the third area, where you're applying a layer of automation to your IG program. We must seek to understand this in-depth.

■■

Strategic Alignment

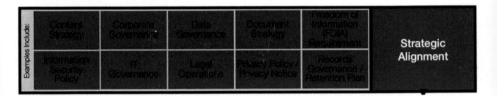

Examples Include:	Content Strategy	Corporate Governance	Data Governance	Document Strategy	Freedom of Information (FOIA) Requirement	Strategic Alignment
	Information Security Policy	IT Governance	Legal Operations	Privacy Policy / Privacy Notice	Records Governance / Retention Plan	

Fig 3.6 MIG (Strategic Alignment stage)

Strategic alignment is about ensuring that your program supports organizational goals and is all-encompassing across all organizational information. Many people like to think of strategic alignment as a one-time activity, which it is, but it's also a practice that you will regularly revisit to stay current with updated organizational goals and to continue to update to meet your organization's information needs. Some organizations bring together their stakeholders on continual evaluation of strategic alignment as frequently as weekly.

In an ideal world, strategic alignment involves reviewing and harmonizing all organizational information policies and practices - in practice, though, many Information Governance programs like the funding to dedicate the time toward the full version of this task and instead, harmonize on a project-by-project basis. While this is currently the prevailing approach, it is not an approach that I'm

PREDISCOVERY

comfortable recommending - it is far riskier to check your policies for a specific project than it is to dedicate the time to reduce the overall risk of contradictory information guidance. That said, if all you can get for executive buy-in is to do this on a project-by-project basis - leverage that mandate as best you can. In this scenario, you can make meaningful progress and generate results by focusing on the highest-results generating project(s) for your organization - then continue to ask for the broader mandate you need to do the complete work when you have an appropriate track record of successes.

When you're aligning your IG program, you look above and below the IG program for existing guidance regarding information. That guidance from above includes your organization's Corporate Governance.

↳ Of Particular Note: Corporate Governance

Information Governance is a high-level discipline, but one area where we take direction (rather than set a direction or harmonize guidance) is Corporate Governance. Corporate Governance rarely includes specificities on the information practices of the organization (barring some notable exceptions) - this is why Information Governance becomes important - it should be a translation of Corporate Governance as it applies to information, specifically.

Corporate Governance is a helpful tool for you in understanding overall organizational direction, understanding the appropriate levels of acceptable risk for the organization, and getting an understanding of the value or importance that the organization places on various parts of the organization - this is often incredibly important in recognizing the likelihood of a full mandate for Information Governance.

In many organizations, upon understanding the Corporate Governance documents, you'll recognize that Information Governance is likely to be an uphill battle, at least in the short term. Many organizations today place very little importance on their most valuable asset, their information - this means that mandates are often challenging to acquire and that often, starting an Information Governance program is simply starting with a small but meaningful project - with hopes of making a greater ask at the end.

Corporate Governance allows us to understand our overall direction and align our IG program with that overall direction. To be clear here, though, while Corporate Governance gives us insights about our organization, it is seldomly simple, and the formats for Corporate Governance documentation vary wildly. When it comes to Corporate Governance, take what you can from the work but don't extrapolate too far from what is clearly articulated until you've also looked at the actual information practices of the organization. The idealistic Corporate Governance is often quite different from the operational information *practices*, with policies also frequently misaligned.

↪ Of Particular Note: Content, Data, Documents, Knowledge, Records, & Everything Else

After you've looked from above at your information through the lens of Corporate Governance, it's time to begin looking from the *other* angles in your organization. Most organizations have multiple disciplines that, in part, have their fiefdoms of information leadership. Your goal is to understand each of your information sub-disciplines (whichever you have within your organization: Content Governance, Content Management, Data Governance, Data Management, Document Management, Document Strategy, Knowledge Management, Knowledge Strategy, Records Governance, Records Management, and any specialized disciplines you may also have [e.g., Document Control, FOIA Processing, CAD Management) from the perspective of policy and practice.

Understanding the sub-disciplines' policies helps you gain a better picture of what the ideal state for that discipline should be. Frequently, policy is divergent from practice, and it is that you'll need to go beyond the policy documents to pursue the actual practice. To get a better understanding of the practices of a sub-discipline, you'll need to ask questions. Depending on your org structure and size, asking questions may be as simple as picking up the phone or as complex as running a survey - use your best judgment on the balance between the invasiveness of questioning and the benefits of the understanding.

You'll repeat this process for every sub-discipline, taking careful notes that will be incredibly helpful for the next stage.

↳ Of Particular Note: Harmonizing

After you've completed your review of policy and practice of the sub-disciplines of Information Governance, now you begin the process of harmonizing. Each organization has a slightly different way of handling this task, but where I've seen the best results is to take a pass at the harmonization project with your core team first, this may be as small as just you. Bring together a list of policies in the sub-disciplines and sort them into policy categories; it may be obvious how to categorize your policies. Still, if you're having difficulties, I'd suggest starting by leveraging the categorization from the ARMA Information Governance Implementation Model (IGIM) - it can serve as an excellent starting point here.

As you bring together your list of policies, you'll often quickly find points of disagreement between the disciplines. Rather than elevate these to full meetings, I like to have simple three-person meetings - as I play the mediator between two leaders of disciplines with conflicting guidance. Often, by seeking to understand one another, one leader will relent and suggest that the other's policy should be prevailing, but in the few cases where I've been unable to find a single solution - only then is the issue elevated to a complete stakeholder discussion. This approach will eliminate awkward discussions in front of an entire group to achieve resolution through an easier path.

Once you've harmonized policies, then it's time to see where your new policies diverge from current practices - and this may be because someone created a new policy or simply because you've found some practices have not been meeting policy objectives.

Helpful list of common documents to find policy statements-

- Content Strategy / Content Management Strategy
- Corporate Governance
- Data Governance
- Document Strategy
- Freedom of Information (FOIA) Requirements (or similar ATIP, FOIP, et al., Requirements)
- Information Security Policy
- IT Governance
- Legal Operations
- Privacy Policy
- Privacy Notice
- Records Governance or Retention / File Plan

Fig. 3.7 Helpful list of common documents to find policy statements

Projects

Legal Holds	Legal Hold Audits	ROT Cleanup & Deduplication	Data Access Governance	PII/PHI Compliant Repositories	
Sensitive Data Access Minimization	Migration & Cleanup	Data Minimization	M&A Due Diligence	Privacy Compliance Audits	**Projects**
Information Security Audits	Assign Ownership for Orphaned Information	Retention Policy Compliance Audit	Industry-Specific Compliance	FOIA / FOIP / ATIP Request Processing	

Fig 3.8 MIG (Projects stage)

After harmonizing policy and strategic alignment, this is the area where improvements begin - there are many types of projects within the realm of Information Governance, and the prioritization of projects should be an accurate reflection of organizational priorities (or you're prioritizing a particular project in response to a negative incident - security breach, privacy lapse, et al.).

Projects can be of the general information improvement variety:

- ROT (redundant, obsolete, and trivial) Cleanup & Deduplication
- Data Minimization
- Migration & Cleanup

Projects may also be in support of improving and ensuring access controls:

- Sensitive Data Access Minimization
- Data Access Governance

Most projects, though, are in support of other information-related disciplines:

- Legal & eDiscovery
    - Legal Holds
    - Legal Hold Audits
    - M&A Due Diligence
- Privacy
    - PCI/PHI/PII Compliant Repositories
    - Privacy Compliance Audits
- Security
    - Assign Ownership for Orphaned Information Assets
    - Information Security Audits
    - Retention Policy Compliance Audits (also valuable for supporting Records Management and Information Management related disciplines)

Lastly, some other projects are specific to particular segments:

- FOIA/FOIP/ATIP (and all other "Right To Know" Laws) Request Processing
- Other Industry-Specific Compliance Reporting

■■

Continuous Improvement (Automation)

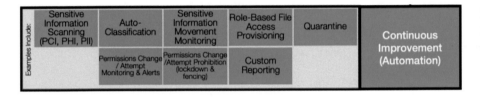

Examples include:	Sensitive Information Scanning (PCI, PHI, PII)	Auto-Classification	Sensitive Information Movement Monitoring	Role-Based File Access Provisioning	Quarantine	Continuous Improvement (Automation)
		Permissions Change / Attempt Monitoring & Alerts	Permissions Change /Attempt Prohibition (lockdown & fencing)	Custom Reporting		

Fig 3.9 MIG (Continuous Improvement-Automation stage)

As Information Governance programs mature, they often begin to apply automation in support of regular activities that frees up (very often limited) human resources to focus on higher-value one-time projects. Likewise, automation also frequently serves as the follow-up to a one-time project - the most common example is a PII (or PCI/PHI) remediation project. In a PII (Personally Identifiable Information) remediation project, you would perform a scan of your various repositories to find PII (the IPRO scanning tool has already been 'trained' on the most common forms of PII). Once your scan is complete, you begin the remediation process, often a combination of redaction and disposition processes. Once your remediation is complete, in the past, that was it - the very next day after you finished your project, there was likely new PII entering your repositories. Today, though, we can apply automation to help solve these challenges on an ongoing basis by automatically scanning across repositories for PII and generating alerts that your information professionals can utilize to continue the process of remediation into the future - keeping your PII issues from continually being an organizational challenge.

There are many areas where automation can be applied (and from an IPRO perspective, we're adding new automation capabilities regularly and constantly having discussions with companies about their application of automation and future desires for automation). I like categorizing things (big surprise there), and when I look at automation, I currently view it as supporting four key areas:

1. Automating organization and access controls
    A. Auto-classification
    B. Role-based file access provisioning
2. Monitoring and Scanning
    A. Sensitive information scanning (PCI, PHI, PII)
    B. Sensitive information movement monitoring
    C. Permissions change/attempt prohibition (both lockdown and fencing)
3. Security automation
    A. Sensitive information movement monitoring [intentionally repeated, as it serves multiple categories]

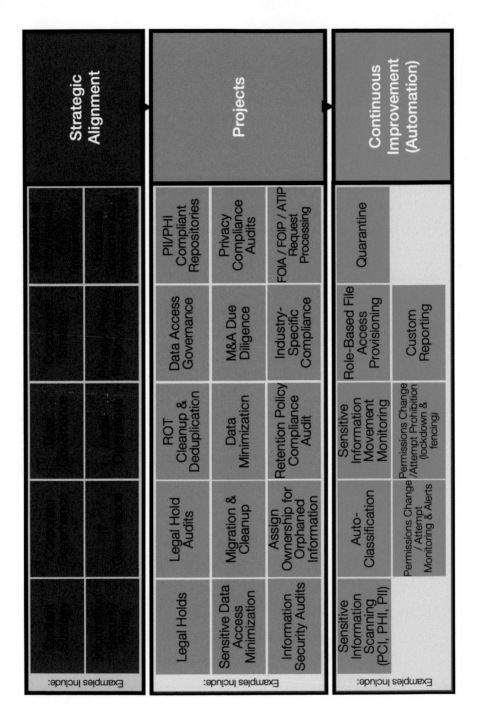

Fig 3.10 MIG

B. Permissions change/attempt prohibition (both lockdown and fencing) [intentionally repeated, as it serves multiple categories]

C. Permissions change/attempt monitoring and alerts

D. Quarantine

4. Report Generation

A. Automated report generation

■■

Information Governance drives prioritization.

There are myriad types of projects and automation that your organization can undertake - the Information Governance team should be driving the prioritization of projects across sub-disciplines to avoid anyone discipline driving their projects forward at the expense of other fields (where the prevailing prioritization should be that of the organization's priorities).

"What is it that the organization most needs?" should become a new mantra, and the previous position of infighting between disciplines that were disconnected (but often competing for the same pool of dollars) should be replaced with collaboration.

■■

Key Takeaways

☐ Many models of Information Governance exist.

☐ EDRM's IGRM is incredibly useful for understanding Information Governance stakeholders.

☐ ARMA's IGIM is incredibly useful for establishing a new Information Governance program.

☐ MIG is incredibly useful for understanding the process of Information Governance.

☐ The IG process can be viewed (in compressed format) as three stages: Strategic Alignment, Projects, Continuous Improvement (Automation).

☐ Strategic Alignment involves reviewing and harmonizing all organizational information policies and practices.

☐ As Information Governance programs mature, they often begin to apply automation.

☐ Information Governance should drive the prioritization of all information projects.

INFORMATION GOVERNANCE FUTURE STATE

Our Collaborative Future

The Future State of Information Governance will be furthering the maturity of Information Governance programs.

At ARMA, we leveraged the model I created, the ARMA IGIM, to survey hundreds of companies regarding their Information Governance maturity[11]. We leveraged those survey results to develop a benchmark for the information governance industry. What we found is that most Information Governance programs are still growing in maturity, and on the 5-point scale (created by Ann K. Snyder during her tenure at ARMA International), most programs today are currently between level 2 (in development) and level 3 (essential). Less than 25% of companies rated themselves a level 4 (proactive) or level 5 (transformational) - this shows a gap between potential and realized benefits

---

[11] [1] ARMA International. "Information Governance Maturity Index Report — 2021." April 2021.

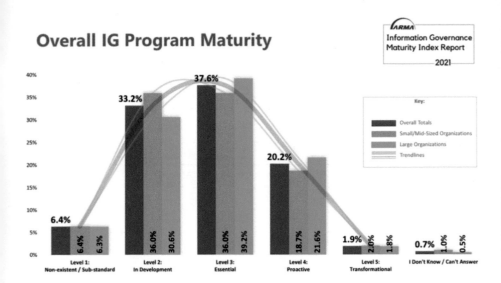

Fig 4.1 ARMA International IG Maturity Index Report 2021 - Overall IG Program Maturity

of Information Governance with less than 2% at level 5 (transformational).

Based on this study, available at https://www.arma.org/igim (the download is free, but you must have an account at ARMA.org), it is my firm belief that the future of Information Governance is slowly arriving, as companies and their employees help to drive Information Governance success (and maturity).

Right now, most companies have taken up the banner of Information Governance, and over the next few years, they will drive new results for their organizations. That there are still companies who haven't adopted IG may also indicate a lack of knowledge or case studies to bolster Information

PREDISCOVERY

Governance efforts - with still, many companies, either in the low end of maturity or simply not within the results as they haven't begun their IG journey yet.

A section on the IG future state then becomes relatively simple: keep maturing, and we'll get there. The groundwork for this stage of our professional growth is complete. We must continue walking the path, realizing benefits, and highlighting our successes - both internally and among executives and publicly - using our profession's bullhorns to share the news that Information Governance is driving tremendous results. Information Governance remains a young profession; your successes, learned and heard, will unleash our collective future.

According to ARMA, the area of greatest weakness in establishing our Information Governance programs is in the area of our Steering Committees (where just 51.1% of respondents declared an acceptable maturity level in this area - as opposed to Infrastructure, the most mature area, coming in at 77.4%).

This area, Steering Committee, our cross-functional connections, across related information disciplines, is where the Information Governance profession is weakest, and where I believe we must put focus in the future.

■■

You Get What You Ask For

Another area that I believe will shape our future in Information Governance is forward-thinking regulation. With GDPR-adjacent legislation working through a patchwork of U.S. states, there are growing calls for federal privacy legislation. I believe that will lead to an eventual overhaul of the information laws of the United States.

In response to this coming need, I've founded InfoGov.net, a new group focused on developing the capacity for lobbying for better information practices in our profession.

■■

Future IG

In the longer term, Information Governance is likely to continue its expansion and importance in organizations of all types. A longer-term vision, though, can get cloudy, especially in a discipline that has been rapidly expanding, has many layers of stakeholders with competing interests, and is likely to benefit from future legislation whose drafts haven't yet seen the light of day. Still, I'll make a few simple predictions that I believe will come to fruition.

■■

↳ Regulation Through Lobbying

I'm someone who started an organization leading lobbying efforts for the broader information profession; it doesn't take that many leaps to know that I believe regulation will be coming and have a massive impact on how organizations of all types, including law firms, handle information. Privacy and security are at the forefront of companies' and firm leadership's concerns - changes in those spaces will be in response to financial pressures or regulation will create financial pressures in response - either way, the future regulatory environment is unlikely to be similar to our current one.

■■

↳ Consumer Grading

The one area where I expect to see Information Governance take a spotlight role is in consumer grading of information safekeeping. Right now, consumers don't know the potential safety of their personal information when they hand it to companies. I can easily see a future of informed risk, where any time a company asks you to submit your personal information, they also must display a rating of their safekeeping capabilities. That rating could be akin to the food safety gradings at NYC restaurants.

■■

Fig 4.2 Common NYC "Sanitary Inspection Grade" signs.

↪ Cyber Insurance Premiums

It has long been my belief that Information Governance has a substantial impact on other information-related disciplines. As new data and surveys show that measurable impact, I believe one area that is likely to respond in kind is insurance.

Actuaries, always seeking indicators that can be used for future *number crunching* will begin measuring IG capabilities as an indicator of cyber insurance risk. This will help premiums move more closely in line with the capabilities and related risks of the underlying organization.

■■

Key Takeaways

- [ ] The future state of Information Governance is furthering the maturity of IG programs.
- [ ] Information Governance will be defined by regulation in the future.
- [ ] Regulation that will impact IG is likely to come in the near future.
- [ ] One vision of what the future of IG may look like is akin to NYC restaurant grading but displaying information handling practices.
- [ ] Future cyber insurance premiums are likely to be looking at Information Governance maturity as a primary decision and pricing factor.

SECTION III: EDISCOVERY

"The best lightning rod for your protection is your own spine." — Ralph Waldo Emerson

EDISCOVERY CURRENT STATE

Two Views

There are two current views of eDiscovery, and who holds each view is dependent on where they're seated within the world of eDiscovery. One hypothesis is that eDiscovery is rapidly becoming incredibly dynamic, with new advanced technologies finding their way into the profession. The other view is that things are static and have remained the same since the paper-based Discovery days.

Both views are correct.

New technologies like Artificial Intelligence (AI) and Machine Learning are gradually being adopted by more companies and firms and presenting an array of intriguing results. Meanwhile, the underlying concepts of the eDiscovery profession have remained chiefly static since George Socha, and Tom Gelbmann released the EDRM model in 2005.

This view of a dynamic profession is growing nearer. The professionals who are leading in the adoption of new technologies tend to view a dynamic profession. Meanwhile, countless lawyers remain on the sidelines for these advancements and continue to perform their role in the law with little change. This dichotomy will not last - those who refuse to adapt are slowly starting to miss out on more prominent corporate cases, and their inability to perform the tasks as rapidly as their competitive firms are beginning to take a toll. Within the next decade, I believe that the laggards will start going out of business (or, more likely, be acquired for their client bases).

■■

Current Process

(What follows is a description of the eDiscovery process, at a high level. If your day-to-day activities are in the world of eDiscovery and this is redundant to you, feel free to skip ahead a few pages.)

The current process underlying eDiscovery is, as has been said, best reflected in the EDRM. To start evaluating how we can build a new model to serve the eDiscovery space (and connect it with Information Governance), we must first understand what process we currently have and give it an honest evaluation.

The current version of the EDRM includes, on the left side, the IGRM or Information Governance Reference Model as a representation of the touchpoints between Information Governance and eDiscovery. We've already segmented out

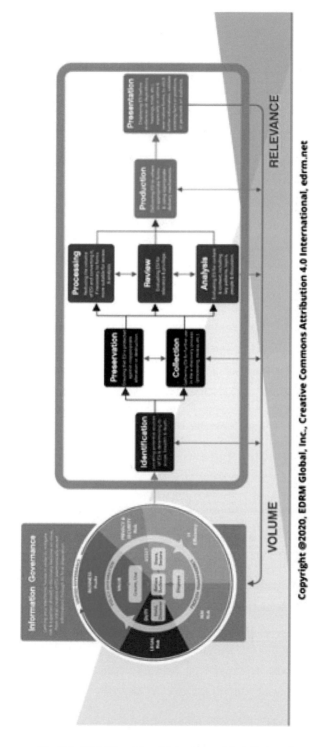

Fig 5.1: EDRM with eDiscovery highlighted

the later addition of the IGRM to look exclusively at the eDiscovery process for this evaluation.

The first step in the EDRM process is "Identification." In the identification stage, one is looking for the various sources related to the subject at hand. These sources can be from individuals, systems, repositories, departments, and more - this stage is to identify areas where relevant information may reside.

The second phase or round in the EDRM process includes both "Preservation" and "Collection." First, we'll address preservation. In the preservation stage, you ensure that the information that has been identified (and later collected) can be saved correctly. Preserving the information means suspending all information destruction or disposition processes. Generally, eDiscovery teams have a preservation plan (Information Governance, IT, or Records departments may execute that plan in conjunction with eDiscovery), and that plan may include multiples steps depending on the organization and the software utilized. An audit trail of the preservation is also required.

The next step in the second phase of the EDRM process is to "Collect." In this stage, the model goes beyond identification and begins to gather actual materials together. This phase starts with strategy, then moves into planning, deciding collection methods, and then actually collecting - even just typing this process out, it is clear that previous professionals in the eDiscovery space built this process for paper or a paper skeuomorph (more on this in Chapter 6 if you're unfamiliar with the term).

The third phase in the EDRM process includes the steps of "Processing," "Review," and "Analysis."

First, "Processing." In this step, we move beyond batches of information and move into the individual pieces of information. From prior stages, digital information may often arrive in various compressed formats like .zip, .pst, .nsf, or .rar, while we must process physical information from boxes, shelves, drawers, or cabinets. We must process these files into individual pieces of information. Further, we must pay careful attention to information metadata - file properties that we must preserve through the processing step for later usage.

Also, within the third phase of EDRM is "Review." Before the exponential increase in organizational information that the PC-era and email brought us, lawyers would review every piece of information for relevance to a case. Today, that expectation is unrealistic and has been unrealistic for decades. In the review stage today, you establish a plan for reviewing (including scope), you put in place your structure for managing reviewers (including training and prep) - in a traditional review, you'd also establish a room for the review. You also plan your review tags, prepare redaction, and prepare your review workflow in this stage. In the review stage, you'll also perform your review and seek to understand the relevancy of information.

Lastly, during this phase is the stage of "Analysis." When EDRM was initially conceived, the Analysis stage was the obvious follow-on from the Review stage - after you review the items, you begin an analysis. Lately, though, the analysis phase has been thought of as more pervasive. Some have advocated that Analysis is a phase that we may enter at any point through the EDRM. That, to me, makes it questionable whether this phase is a catch-all for activities that usually fall under the realm of Information Governance. If anything, the lack of consistent reading of the model[12] shows that the model may not have changed, but the professionals' activities are changing - where they're going next, that is what I am looking to define in our coming chapters.

The following phase has but one stage within it, "production." In this stage, parties agree to a schedule for production, all production requirements including file formats and production forms (native, near-native, image, or paper), load file type (if load file), bates number requirements (if any), stamping requirements (if any), redaction requirements (if any), and the media type/online delivery.

Finally, the final phase in the EDRM model also includes but one stage, "present." In this stage, lawyers display

---

[12] as evidenced by EDRM's quote of "When the model was originally conceived, the focus was on the analysis of the collected documents to make it easier to cull documents and provide increased productivity during the review step. More recently, all types of analytics are being used to increase productivity through the whole process." - https://edrm.net/resources/frameworks-and-standards/edrm-model/analysis/

information as exhibits at depositions, hearings, trials, etc., to, according to EDRM, "elicit further information, validate existing facts or positions, or persuade an audience.[13]

That is the current state of eDiscovery processes in an abbreviated form (with just enough detail that we can endeavor to reimagine the process and improve our shared professions). Later, we will discuss the unquantified insights you can gain during the eDiscovery process and how capturing those insights can create massive benefits for companies while providing a new competitive advantage for law firms and legal service providers. For example, when an eDiscovery professional encounters a batch of documents that contain personally identifiable information (PII) during a review, what should happen with that insight? More on that as we bring together eDiscovery and Information Governance disciplines in Chapters 8 and 9.

■■

Key Takeaways

☐ New technologies are greatly impacting eDiscovery.
☐ Underlying processes for eDiscovery are largely still based on paper.

---

[13] https://edrm.net/resources/frameworks-and-standards/edrm-model/presentation-guid/

- [ ] Companies are largely outsourcing cost containment measures to outside law firms or service providers.
- [ ] Paper based processes must be replaced with current, digital-first processes.
- [ ] Massive file transfers are frequent in the eDiscovery process but pose a significant source of security and privacy risk.

EDISCOVERY PROCESS EVALUATION

A Skeuomorphic Process

As explained above in detail and readily apparent in the evaluation of the EDRM, paper-based Discovery is still at the heart of most of the underlying processes of eDiscovery.

Skeuomorphism, or the designing of digital representation of physical objects (the most common example is the "save icon" looking exactly like a 3.5" floppy disk - an item we no longer use for saving), is generally discussed in the context of an individual entity or object. In the case of eDiscovery, we have a skeuomorphic process - the whole process was derived initially from paper-based processes. It is this skeuomorphism that we must shed if we're to bring eDiscovery into the 21st Century.

■■

We Live In A Digital World

In a digital world, we scan paper and bring those scans into our eDiscovery process - we must, in this world, ditch the paper addiction fully and completely. For some readers, this may have been something you did quite a while ago, but rest assured, there are many people who still today need to ditch their paper habit.

In a digital world, we don't need to think of processes as single steps - we can layer steps on top of one another. In fact, the first three steps of the eDiscovery portion of the EDRM could be described as, searching through a file room to *identify*, pulling papers out and putting them into your own folder to *collect* them, then walking down the hall and handing off to a Records Manager or Paralegal to *preserve* them. Unlike paper that would need to be walked down a hall for a process to continue, one button push in the digital world can mean more than one action has taken place. We're going to drive eDiscovery forward - not by reinventing eDiscovery, but by decoupling our process from tree corpses (paper) and understanding that we now must live in a digital world.

■■

Killing Collection

In the collection phase, we bring together information. Today, we can look to other stages to select input and double up on our process. In this case, for collection, we can look to the phase of Analyze - as information is analyzed, at two potential areas where the collection could happen in the background: either right at the start as we "Identify" or later when we "Analyze." I believe that collection should occur automatically behind the scenes, which should happen during the Analyze phase. Since one of our aims is to reduce massive file transfers, moving collection later will reduce the amount of information involved in transfers and push transfers. Again, this isn't paper - we can perform more than one task at a time on a digital file and gain efficiency, so we should!

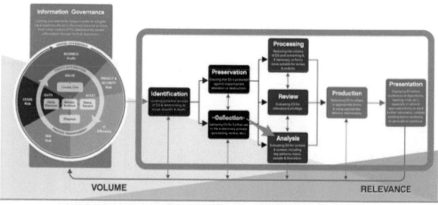

Fig 6.1: EDRM with modernization stage 1

Punting Preservation

Preservation is another process step that I believe we can fold into another part of our process. Preservation, putting information on legal hold, should happen at the earliest stage of the process and protect relevant information from deletion or change - and as we find information to be not relevant, the system should automatically release the legal hold. All of this should be pretty easily automated but must start with a process step. We can move preservation to happen during collection, the very first step. There is no reason that when you first cast your net for relevant information that your software should preserve all of that potentially pertinent and responsive information.

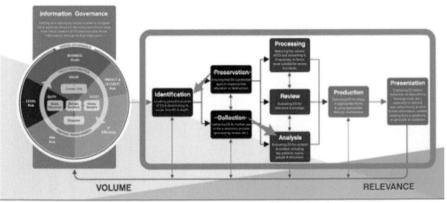

Fig 6.2: EDRM with modernization stage 2

PREDISCOVERY

■■

Passing Processing

According to EDRM, in processing, we perform "actions on ESI (Electronically Stored Information) to allow for metadata preservation, itemization, normalization of format, and data reduction via selection for review." Each of these steps we can automate today according to best practice (and through settings panels). Through greater consistency in information handling (how many times must we discuss how we want to produce an Excel file?) and a greater reliance on Artificial Intelligence and Machine Learning (both technologies now more widely available), the processing is another step that we can shift. Some processing will be required in the early stage of Identification (spot checking files and quality assurance), while the rest can be withheld until later in the process, during the Analyze phase, helping you utilize your system resources more effectively in this process.

Five steps remain within a new eDiscovery process, although we haven't addressed how to reduce our massive file transfers.

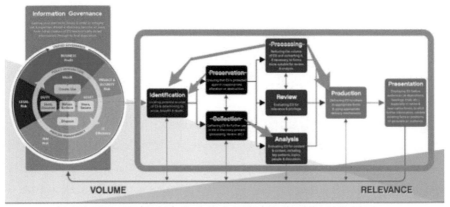

Fig 6.3: EDRM with modernization stage 3

■■

Reducing Massive File Transfers

In most other business processes completed in conjunction with partners, the primary company (the client) generally retains all information. In eDiscovery, it is the opposite - this is a massive privacy and security concern. It is also the reason why law firms remain a top target for hackers.

To solve eDiscovery, we simply look to other processes outside our realm and how different approaches dealt with similar issues. In each of these solutions, there are two common threads:

1. Users at the partner organization have accounts provisioned so that the client organization retains all access controls.

2. The client can limit information access by the partner organization.

Limited and provisioned access is how other industries connect to their partners and allow for access - this too should be our approach, at least in the early stages.

■■

Key Takeaways

☐ eDiscovery is a skeuomorphic process with Discovery as its physical analog.

☐ Digital processes can perform more efficiently than paper-based processes.

☐ By looking through a lens of efficiency and efficacy, the eDiscovery process can be greatly simplified.

☐ Many are currently reevaluating massive file transfers related to eDiscovery and a pathway of limited and provisioned access is the likely path forward.

EDISCOVERY PROCESS FUTURE STATE

A Vision for the Future

In reimagining the eDiscovery process, we eliminated multiple steps by simply moving that stage's activities in line with other stages - this is a digital world, so we can drive efficiency in ways that we never could with paper. That leaves us with five steps and a mechanism for "limited and provisioned" information access.

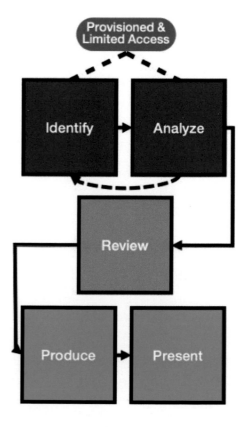

Fig 7.1: Building a new model

■■

Limited & Provisioned Access: Live EDA

In the IPRO world, we've created that limited and provisioned access - we call it Live EDA, and our clients have just recently started using the feature. How it works is that a company can provide secure access to its law firm or service provider. That will give the law firm or service provider limited access directly into live information repositories (or portions thereof) without the ability to affect or change any of that underlying information (or related metadata).

That view works across your various repositories, allowing you to follow the chain of actions as they move between systems – e.g. a chat in Microsoft Teams, leads to an email, leads to a collaboratively created document with 3 authors, leads to a signed version of that document that's a contract sitting in a Records system (probably with 15 other copies in various email boxes and other systems).

Through one view, you can better understand the context of your information and start to flip the EDRM process to drive relevance through a rapid Identify-Analyze recursive process. The one view allows for a process that looks more like the one on the following page.

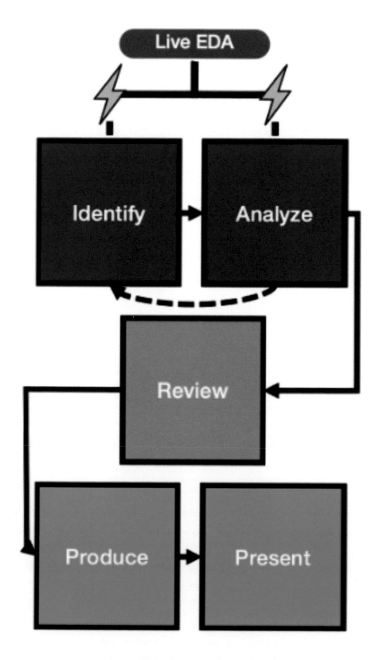

Fig 7.2: IPRO eDiscovery Model 1.0

Working with Partners

Throughout the entirety of the eDiscovery process, there are options on how the company leverages outside partners - law firms, legal service providers, software vendors, consultants. You must make partnership decisions based on your risk tolerance and business practices (see Fig 7.3).

Often there are partner "ecosystems" where there may be existing relationships between partners with aligned expertise or goals. In those partner ecosystems, there can also be a variety of expertise that can be leveraged that go beyond simply eDiscovery - many cross-functional practices may stretch into compliance, privacy, security, records, IT, and other information-related disciplines, or even at the higher level of Information Governance.

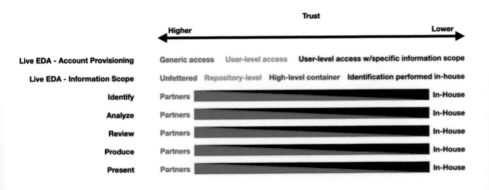

Fig 7.3: Working with Partners

Reducing risk doesn't equate to eliminating risk, and in some areas we must seek to make , and with Live EDA, we are reducing the risk of transferring large volumes of information from a company to its partners. Instead, this new model relies on provisioned and limited access, so decisions must be made around account provisioning and limiting access to information.

■■

Live EDA Account Provisioning

In the future, I believe that all companies will use some type of provisioning of user-level accounts for their partners. That said, many companies, instead, provide generic accounts (usually group or company-based) instead of user-specific accounts. In a generic account model, neither the company nor the partner(s) will be able to use log files to determine which specific individuals performed which activities on a particular case (not recommended), but one could utilize the log file to see which partner (at the partner company level) performed which tasks. Depending on your organization's level of trust and business requirements related to logs, you can decide how you will provide information access for your partners.

■■

Live EDA Information Scoping

It is possible to limit the provisioned Live EDA accounts to any information scope- from full, unfettered access to all organizational information through to individual pieces of information assigned to a specific user account. Most organizations find themselves somewhere in the middle of these two options - but it is an open conversation that the company must have with their partner(s).

■■

Identify

Let's work through an example in this new model. A recent case arrives, and the first step is to identify. During identifying information, anything that is potentially relevant should be collected and put on legal hold automatically. Some eDiscovery software forces you into legacy information collection models- gathering everything potentially pertinent to your case (and usually storing that information in the eDiscovery software, generating lucrative storage fees). At IPRO, we took a different approach, one that puts our clients' needs first. Our software gives you an alternative approach that we believe will be the future path forward in eDiscovery - simply focusing on what's relevant.

Instead of collecting large pools of information, look to leverage our Active Learning and Live EDA capabilities to focus on finding what's truly relevant- leveraging the power of Artificial Intelligence and Machine Learning to get you to the information you need. You can do this by leveraging Active Learning.

Active Learning is about leveraging software to automate portions of the eDiscovery process, namely, Identification and Analysis. In Active Learning, the software, based on software "training" provided by IPRO or performed by your team, identifies potentially relevant content to your matter and leverages human intervention only on items where the software is less sure of relevance. The goal of this approach is to drive efficiency.

You can also do this by leveraging additional capabilities like automated AI-based information clustering - leveraging the AI to group information to make your review of that information much faster and easier.

Rather than going through every piece of information individually, we can leverage clustering to pursue relevance. By leveraging Machine Learning, IPRO clusters together similar information into groupings – which you can then click through to find what is relevant. In addition to its use in eDiscovery, this is often a technique used by Auditors and Internal Investigations teams.

This clustering results in a visual representation we call the Concept Wheel. This visual approach allows you to take visual cues and provides an alternate or additional method to pursue relevant information.

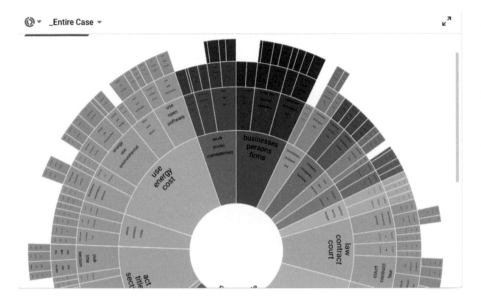

Fig 7.4: Concept wheel example

In addition to new concepts, classic methods of Collection remain available as well.

Lastly, every project phase likely should include some kind of quality assurance, so during the identify phase, you'll likely spot-check the work, which may require some basic information processing (e.g., an unviewable format is made readable). In addition to new concepts, classic methods of Collection remain available as well.

■■

A Note on Legal Holds

Legal holds are applied when a case or a "reasonable expectation of litigation" triggers a duty to preserve. Legal holds prevent the regular disposition or deletion of information that is likely to be required in litigation. There are two approaches to legal holds, and IPRO supports either direction. Neither approach is perfect, so it's essential to understand the techniques to decide which is correct, either for your organization (generally) or your specific case.

■■

The Snapshot Approach

In the snapshot approach, items are selected and placed on legal hold by making a copy in a safe location. This approach aims not to put things on legal hold within their original systems - a commonly desired path, but one that can lead to inconsistencies between information repositories that may or may not have the capabilities (or the *same* capabilities for consistency's sake) for legal holds. In the snapshot approach, we save a copy of all items under hold in IPRO software. This approach eliminates a few issues present in the in-place legal hold process:

1. Most companies use multiple information repositories (email, collaborative platforms, shared drives, and information systems of all varieties), and the native legal hold process in each of those systems can present inconsistencies.

2. Inconsistencies in legal hold processes present inconsistent results - inconsistent results are not viewed positively by the courts.

3. Employees of the organization do not need (and in most cases, probably should have) visibility into the organization's legal actions. Putting items on legal hold in native systems can be an indicator to employees of legal action.

In response to those challenges, we support the snapshot approach to applying legal holds, all centralized within our software - separated from the rest of your organizational information. Applying information holds in this method is consistent no matter which systems the information resides within (even between email, shared drives, collaborative platforms [like Slack or Teams], and full-fledged information systems).

Lastly, using the snapshot approach reduces visibility and makes legal holds a 'need to know' item that stays within the legal department.

The In-Place Hold Approach

In the In-Place legal hold approach, you prevent the deletion or disposition of pieces of information WITHIN the native system where the information resides (e.g., if a Word file resides within a Microsoft SharePoint environment, you prevent the disposition or deletion of the item within Microsoft SharePoint and the item remains in place). This approach is preferable for organizations with a limited number of primary information systems where the capabilities of those systems are similar (and meet your organizational needs for legal holds). Today this remains much rarer than professionals realize, with many asking for in-place hold then, upon looking at requirements, reverting to a snapshot approach. There are numerous benefits for those in pursuit of the in-place approach if you can utilize the method successfully in your information environment.

The benefits of the in-place hold approach are:

1. Keeping information in place in native systems prevents additional copies of your files from being created within your network (as the snapshot approach does).
2. In-place legal holds prevent the legal department from having information repositories that they must maintain.
3. The in-place legal holds approach is minimally disruptive to the organization as the information continues to

PREDISCOVERY

reside where it originally lived (and employees can still utilize that information).

■■

The IPRO Approach to Legal Holds

The IPRO approach to legal holds is to meet you where you are and provide you options that can work for you in whatever scenario is most beneficial for your organization. While some eDiscovery vendors force you into one approach or the other, snapshot or in-place, we've made forward progress on legal holds by offering you the flexibility you need to meet your needs. If you aren't leveraging IPRO for your legal holds function, ensure that your system applies consistent legal holds in light of the above.

■■

Analyze

After Identifying the large, potentially responsive pools of information, we begin to Analyze. After processing, this is a natural flow - you've identified the large pools, cast a wide net, and automatically applied legal holds. Now, you begin determining your path forward - making decisions that will propel the case onward.

Here you'll estimate the amount of information to be preserved based on the initial collection (or you'll *know* what information will be held by taking one of the more modern paths for collection - Active Learning, AI, and Machine Learning.

This approach makes it easier to predict costs, assess legal strategies, and evaluate discovery scenarios. Once these decisions and predictions are complete, the litigation team can prepare for their next steps: a meet and confer or settlement conference.

■■

Review

Logically, the next step is to perform the full review - this is increasingly a task performed by partners. Review essentially looks the same in this next phase of the evolution of eDiscovery as it did in the last phase. In the review stage, you still establish a plan for reviewing (including scope), you set your structure for managing reviewers (including training and preparation). You also plan your review tags, prepare redaction, and prepare your review workflow in this stage. In the review stage, you'll also perform your review, apply AI and advanced technology to help, and seek to understand the relevancy of information (IPRO has many unique features to help you move through the review stage efficiently).

■■

Produce

Before producing information, you'll want to confirm the methods/formats of production: a schedule for production, all production requirements including file formats and production forms (native, near-native, image, or paper), load file type (if load file), bates number requirements (if any), stamping requirements (if any), redaction requirements (if any), and the media type/online delivery. Then you execute and produce in the agreed-upon methods/formats.

When both parties are using IPRO, this is incredibly easy using the native capabilities of the software. When opposing parties use software other than IPRO, we still support you by supporting most standard output formats.

■■

Present

And, again, lastly, "present." In this new process for eDiscovery, Presentation remains essentially the same. Lawyers display information as exhibits at depositions, hearings, trials, etc., to, again, according to EDRM, "elicit further information, validate existing facts or positions, or persuade an audience."[14]

IPRO stands essentially alone among eDiscovery vendors in providing end-to-end solutions, *including* trial presentation. IPRO TrialDirector software remains the leading software for displaying evidence in trial.

■■

The Relevance First [RF] Approach

We've already uncovered the ways that traditional eDiscovery is changing today. Still, there's also another movement afoot today that's also drastically shifting the conventional approaches to eDiscovery, and that's the "Relevance First" (RF) movement, which seems poised to have its day soon.

---

[14] https://edrm.net/resources/frameworks-and-standards/edrm-model/presentation-guid/

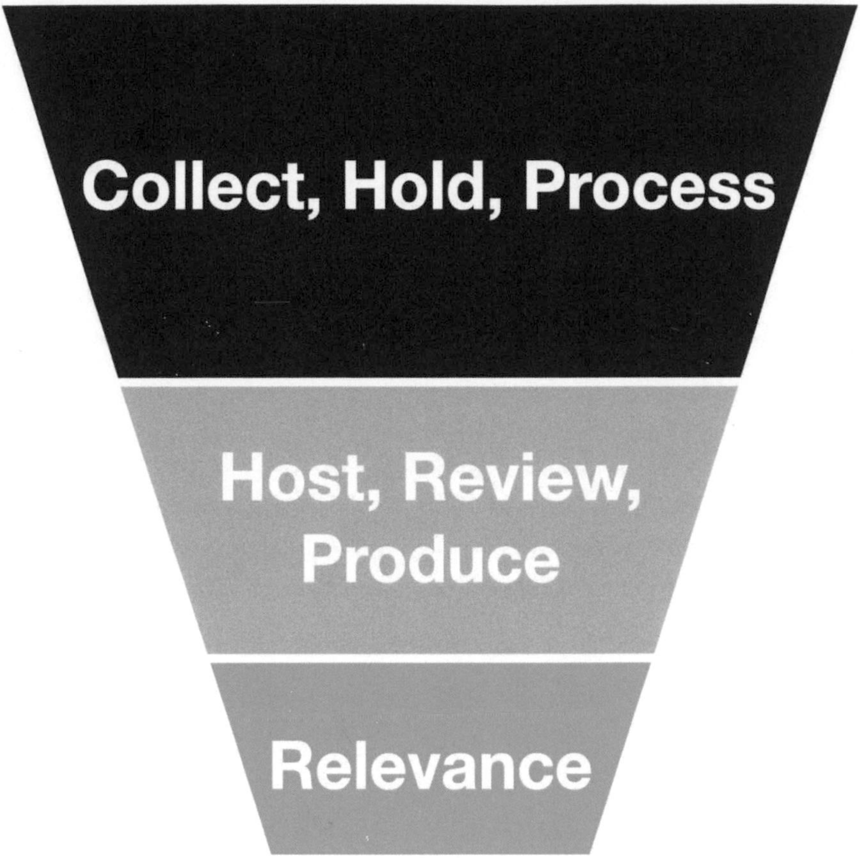

Fig 7.5 A traditional "funnel" approach

Deeply reliant on advanced technologies (Artificial Intelligence [AI] and Machine Learning [ML], of which Active Learning [AL] is a subset), this new Relevance First approach aims to flip the entire eDiscovery approach on its head.

Our approaches to eDiscovery, no matter their specific workflow, has always been based around the general concept that we collect information that we think could be relevant to a case, then we cull down and filter our way to what's truly relevant. The typical picture of a funnel is what we've always utilized (see fig 7.5).

There's always been this deep-held fantasy that one day our technology may become so advanced that it can infer context and deliver the information relevant to a matter. Well, that day, some say, is here.

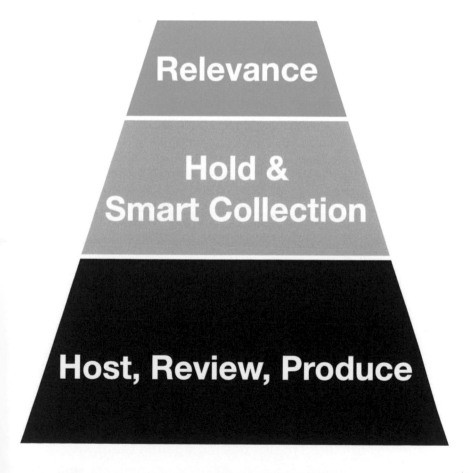

Fig 7.6 A sample of a "Relevance First" (RF) approach.

It'll still take some convincing that RF is a concept that we should utilize for all cases, but it's hard to argue with results. Certainly, right now, we shouldn't yet do massive enterprise cases through an RF approach unless there's an obvious "smoking gun." That said, as an alternate pathing for existing cases (to take a look at a case using different techniques to find potential differences or determine which approach will serve the matter best) or as a way to handle simple routine cases, it may be time for RF to receive its moment - because, well, it works and it's easy to understand - that's a recipe for wildfire-like adoption (fig 7.6).

In an RF approach, one would start by finding one piece of information relevant to the case through search, advanced search, or other means. From there, the technology enhances the human's ability to determine relevance - by branching off of one piece of relevant information to the case. To this end, the technology provides suggestions of additional relevant information, often involving human guidance, but one could foresee a future not far off where that would be less necessary for simple cases.

Progress toward achieving RF success is much nearer than many of us realize. Our entire way of performing eDiscovery is likely to shift once again or have the potential to branch into two kinds of eDiscovery - one for simple, routine cases that leverages technology and RF; another for advanced and complex issues relying more on humans and more traditional approaches.

Only time will tell, but I'm not betting against team RF.

Key Takeaways

☐ In a digital-first process, you can drive efficiency in ways we never could with paper.

☐ Limited and provisioned access has been envisioned in IPRO's Live EDA.

☐ Working with partners is an exercise in risk tolerance and alignment of business practices.

☐ Partner "ecosystems" may be helpful when they are expansive and collaborative.

☐ The future is likely to include some type of account provisioning, like IPRO's Live EDA.

☐ Information scoping is an approach to risk reduction with partners.

☐ There are now many new techniques for identification of information that rely on advanced technologies that didn't previously exist.

☐ Legal holds can be applied in two approaches: the snapshot approach or the in-place approach.

☐ Snapshot approach ensures consistency but creates potential duplication.

☐ In-place approach may not be consistent between many different platforms but doesn't create duplicates or storage fees.

☐ Analyzing information can be achieved more easily through active learning, AI, and Machine Learning techniques.

☐ Review is a step increasingly performed by partners leveraging advanced technology approaches with human capital.

☐ The Relevance First [RF] approach seeks to disrupt the process of eDiscovery by seeking relevant information first, finding a piece, then pursuing related information across information systems to achieve a similar result to eDiscovery.

☐ Relevance First [RF] approaches are gaining traction rapidly.

SECTION IV: ALIGNMENT & A NEW MODEL FOR eDISCOVERY & INFORMATION GOVERNANCE

"The future is always beginning now." - Mark Strand

BRINGING THE DISCIPLINES TOGETHER

Interdisciplinary Bridges

The future state for Information Governance and eDiscovery, I believe, takes advantage of interdisciplinary bridges that may or may not exist. If you're starting anew, a great place to start is to start with your internal partnerships with information sub-disciplines - as the future of Information Governance and eDiscovery is going to be ever more powered by these connections.

In evaluating our current state of Information Governance, it is clear that there are deep connections between Information Governance and its partner sub-disciplines - the evident learning from me and driving our team at IPRO forward is how to better leverage those partnerships for further advancement.

■■

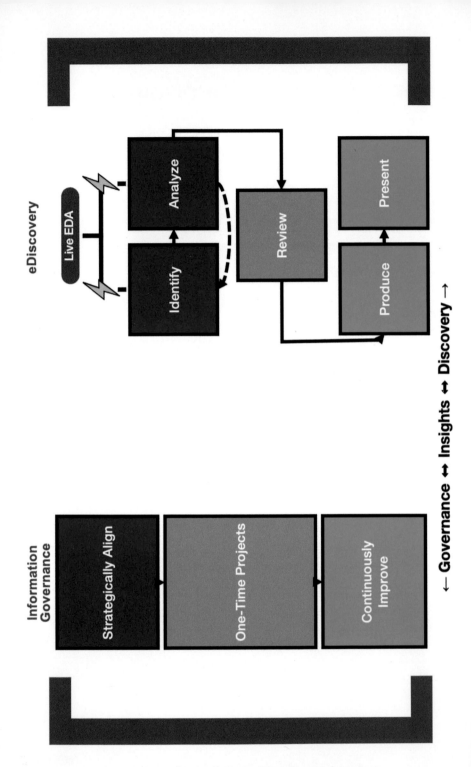

Fig 8.1 The two disciplines beside one another.

Passive Insight Capture

We believe you can achieve new benefits and drive the future of Information Governance through the concept of Passive Insight Capture (PIC). PIC is how we leverage the partnerships between disciplines and move Information Governance forward. At IPRO, we've developed a Passive Insight Capture loop between Information Governance and eDiscovery by leveraging IPRO tools in both fields to drive advancement in both.

In our previous chapters, we have already established that we had sought to view eDiscovery and Information Governance in the context of the process - and having developed a process-oriented view of Information Governance in the MIG. When we align these two processes, we start to identify a new pathway between the disciplines - one that has yet to be taken, insights.

In our image of the profession (fig 8.1), we see Information Governance at the left, eDiscovery at the right, and a gap between the disciplines that we're labeling "Insights."

On the eDiscovery side, things continue in this new version of the model - as we're seeing with our early adopting clients, the process moves a bit faster after our efficacy and efficiency reengineering. This new way of thinking uses five steps in a primarily linear direction, as opposed to 8 steps that are non-linear of the classic EDRM.

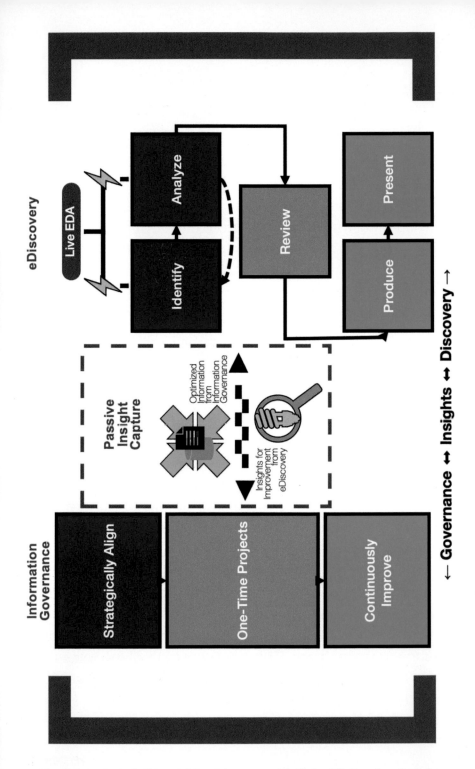

Fig 8.2 MIGeD (MIG + IPRO eDiscovery Model with Passive Insight Capture loop

Through this process, there are often insights that we could capture but currently do not. The Review process serves as a great point of contact with an organization's information - you have people reviewing individual pieces of information. Right now, reviewers (in most cases) are looking for three things - items responsive to the particular case, items unresponsive to the specific case, and items of privilege (attorney-client). However, the reality is that reviewers often find **other** valuable things: PII, PCI, PHI, ROT, duplicate items, and so much more. The problem, though, while these findings are potentially helpful for the organization, they're not beneficial for the process that the reviewer is going through: namely, review for a case.

That's where the software must step in. Through Passive Insight Capture (see Fig 8.2), we apply AI and Machine Learning behind-the-scenes of the review process, and we leverage the reviewer as a validator of findings.

In the eDiscovery review process, we capture "insights" - and where do those insights go? They become remediation alerts for the professionals leveraging the Information Governance portion of our software.

Through Passive Insight Capture, we're able to collect insights through the eDiscovery process (without adding or changing the process) and deliver those crucial insights to the Information Governance professional who can use their process (usually a "one-time project") to act upon the PIC alert.

The result of this Passive Insight Capture loop is to drive optimization of the information environment. Without changing how people interact with information - we've created a new improvement point between the disciplines.

By improving the eDiscovery process and tying in the Information Governance process, we're able to unlock a myriad of benefits:

- drive faster results in eDiscovery (through the improved process)
- monetary savings from faster eDiscovery (through the improved process)
- monetary savings from better browse/search times across an organization
- monetary savings from ongoing information environment optimization (by leveraging PIC)
- faster relevance in eDiscovery through continuous information environment optimization (by leveraging PIC)
- leverage a new source to drive improvements in Information Governance (PIC alerts)

As we're starting to see our early adopter clients take advantage of this new way of driving information optimization and improvement, we are bolstered in our belief that this is the path forward: together.

Key Concepts

☐ We need to build the interdisciplinary bridges between eDiscovery and Information Governance.

☐ Passive Insight Capture is a process for driving further advancement out of the eDiscovery process by looking beyond case boundaries towards the identification of information deficiencies.

A NEW MODEL FOR EDISCOVERY & INFORMATION GOVERNANCE

The IPRO Unified Information Governance-eDiscovery Model

A new model for eDiscovery is one that, like EDRM before it, recognizes the need for Information Governance and as laid out in this book, must learn from it. A new model must not only be effective, but must also drive efficiency. Our new model must be forward-looking and aspirational, so that it can serve us long into the future.

It is my honor to present the results of our dissection of eDiscovery and Information Governance, a new set of models: the Unified Model, MIG, & IPRO eDiscovery Model.

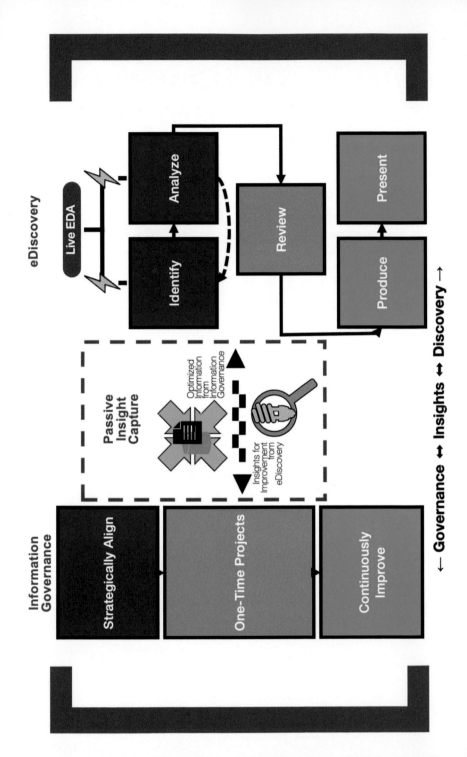

Fig 9.1: The Unified Model (MIG + IPRO eDiscovery Model with PIC)

Fig 9.2: MIG - Compressed View

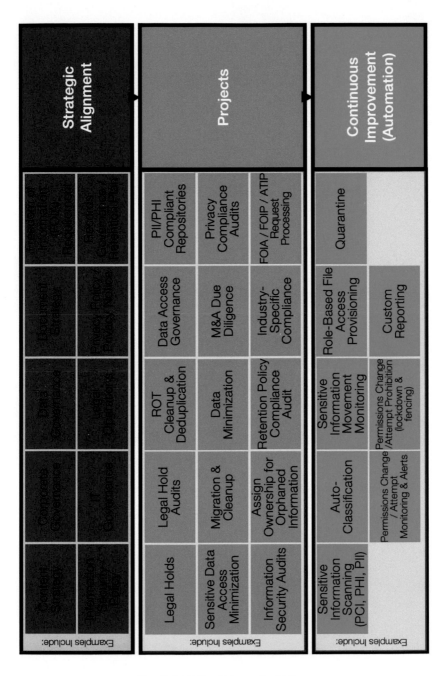

Fig 9.3 MIG - Expanded View

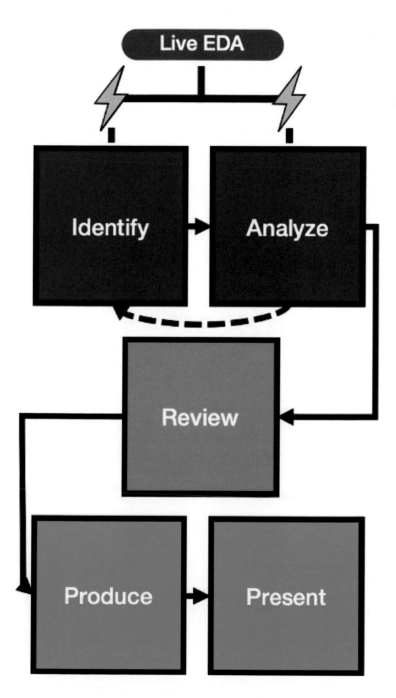

Fig 9.4 The IPRO eDiscovery Model

Additional Resources

Download high resolution images, slides that you can easily utilize in presentations or meetings, document templates to help you along the way, and a reader community at

https://myigl.ink/prediscovery

Conclusion

In my other role as the Director of Information Governance at IPRO, I've been very fortunate to have been given the mandate to create change in the future of the information profession through our software offerings. As such, we're able to explore and examine, determine the best path forward, then develop the tools that will help move you and our professions forward.

With the advancements outlined in this book, I believe we provide an advantage to those willing to drive progress on this new path.

The futures of both the eDiscovery and Information Governance fields are brightest when we are able to drive progress together.

ABOUT THE AUTHOR: NICK INGLIS

Nick Inglis is both the Director of Information Governance at IPRO and Founder of InfoGov.net (where he is also the Host of The Strategy of Information podcast). Inglis was formerly Executive Director, Content & Programming at ARMA International (through the acquisition of the Information Coalition and Information Governance Conference, where Inglis served as President). Before Co-Founding and leading the Information Coalition, Mr. Inglis served as the Director of Professional Development at AIIM and was an Assistant Vice President at Bank of America.

Inglis is the author of two previous books 'INFORMATION: The Comprehensive Overview of the Information Profession' and 'The AIIM SharePoint 2010 Governance Toolkit'. His other writing has been featured in U.S. News & World Report, The Providence Journal, Yahoo! Finance, CMSWire, and others. When not adding to his collection of certificates and certifications (CIP, IGP, INFO, ERMm, SharePointm, BPMm, E2.0m, ECMm, IMCP), he is likely spending time with his son, Conor Atom, and wife, Deanna.

In addition to his work with the information profession, Inglis has also led public advocacy campaigns. He worked with Providence Student Union on ushering a subsidized college proposal through the RI State House – leading Rhode Island to offer tuition-free community college to every graduating high school student; he also ushered a proposal to establish Net Neutrality at the state level in RI through an Executive Order from then-Governor Gina Raimondo.